THE GRASSROOTS GUIDE
TO
Saving What Matters

HISTORIC PRESERVATION FOR EVERYDAY PEOPLE

BETH YARBROUGH

Copyright © 2025 by Beth Yarbrough

All rights reserved. This book may not be reproduced or stored in whole or in part by any means without the written permission of the author except for brief quotations for the purpose of review.

ISBN: 978-1-966343-21-9 (soft cover)

Yarbrough. Beth
Edited by: Amy Ashby

Cover image by Beth Yarbrough.
The photo is of the Bellamy Mansion in Wilmington, North Carolina.

Warren Publishing
Charlotte, NC
www.warrenpublishing.net
Printed in the United States

INTRODUCTION

This book is for anybody who cares about saving old structures, whether valued historically, architecturally, culturally, or sentimentally. Serving as a layperson's road map through the preservation landscape, this guide can be used by individuals, groups of concerned citizens, nonprofits, and other entities seeking to learn how better to protect the historic structures in their communities.

I am just like most of you, a private citizen who cares deeply about saving the historic structures in our midst. I am not professionally trained, but rather an armchair enthusiast. Even so, across a decade of traveling the country and encountering many sad cases of endangered structures, I have learned a few things—not the least of which is the fact that there is a lot of help available, but the public's awareness of that help and how it works is lagging way behind. My goal with this book is to change that dynamic.

Beth Yarbrough

TABLE OF CONTENTS

Chapter 1: I Wish Someone Would Save That Place 1

Chapter 2: Is It Really Protected? 7

Chapter 3: Why Bother? 13

Chapter 4: Where Can I Find Help? 16

Chapter 5: Grants and Incentives 20

Chapter 6: I Just Want to Save My House 25

Chapter 7: We Meant Well 29

Chapter 8: I Just Want to Save My Town 36

Chapter 9: Strength in Numbers 40

Chapter 10: More than One Way to Stop a Bulldozer 45

Chapter 11: The Art of Win-Win 49

Chapter 12: If Europe Can Do It 52

Chapter 13: What Now? 54

Chapter 14: Save This List 57

1
I WISH SOMEONE WOULD SAVE THAT PLACE
How Old Houses Die

Death is often a complicated process for an old house. Like many of you, I have found myself watching the relentless march of an old place toward the inevitable and wondered how such a thing could be allowed to happen. Through the years, I have asked questions and discovered not one or two but dozens of reasons why so many old houses fall by the wayside.

We're going to take a look at those reasons in this chapter. A better understanding of how old houses die is the first step toward understanding how to save them.

> A better understanding of how old houses die is the first step toward understanding how to save them.

Stubborn Defiance

Not all abandoned or endangered properties are the fault of the property owners themselves, and we will get to that in a moment. There are, however, a good number of these situations that are the result of stubborn defiance.

The first example is a situation involving a property with more than one owner, as when a former homeplace is bequeathed to all of the surviving children as a collective group. In many of these situations, decisions about how to move forward with the property have to be unanimous, and if there is one holdout, then the rest of the group is left powerless. They cannot sell unless everyone is in agreement. To be sure, the issue of estates and how they are legally constructed can vary widely, and there may be remedies in some that prevent situations like this. Also, to be fair, disputes among heirs do not always involve clear-cut good guys and bad guys. But in the case of old houses, very often the one holdout causes years of delay, during which the property goes downhill.

The second example is a property with one stubborn and defiant owner who simply will not sell because he or she does not want to, even though there have been repeated offers. This type of defiant personality is not open to reason—even when the obvious plight of the structure is undeniable. Sometimes this has to do with an owner unwilling to let go of the land underneath a structure, but other times it has to do with pure "meanness," as we say in the South. Either way, the lone-wolf stubborn owner is a tough situation.

Denial
This situation is a first cousin to Stubborn Defiance, but Denial hangs its hat on a specific reason for not wanting to sell. In these cases, unrealistic owners believe they will be able to restore the place "someday." Others have self-esteem issues that depend heavily on being the owner of something significant or historic, even if it is obviously getting ready to collapse.

One example of Denial was the farmer in rural New Jersey who steadfastly refused for years to sell a significant old Greek Revival farmhouse to a good friend of mine, saying that he had plans to restore the place. Several years later, Hurricane Sandy came along and reduced the whole thing to a pile of splinters, the farmer never having lifted the first finger.

As well, there was the house in Eastern North Carolina missing half its roof, daylight streaming down into what was once the living room. A neighbor told us that the owner was in the process of renovating, even though he hadn't been there in years. There was a faded building permit tacked to the front door that had expired nine years prior. A few counties away, another significant old house stood with the same issues, belonging to an owner who refused discussion about selling for the same reason—"We're planning to restore"—even when sent a photo of a hole in the roof that had been there two years and was the size of a car.

These are not the only examples, sad to say. Denial is a huge contributor to the demise of old houses.

Financial Strain and Extenuating Circumstances
We cannot always, however, ascribe blame for endangered properties to owners who don't care. I learned a tender and heartbreaking lesson a few years ago when I posted on social media about a gorgeous old Victorian house that appeared abandoned and was overgrown and desperately in need of attention. While I always try to be sensitive when posting about these old places, I did observe that this place could use some love. An hour after the post was published, I received a message from the owner. She was living in the house under extreme financial strain, desperate to find a way to keep up a home that had been in her family for generations, her heart in her throat at the sad state of the house, terrified that it might pass out of her family forever.

This is a sad but not uncommon situation with a good number of endangered houses. Many are owned by families with no resources who would certainly take care of the places if they could afford to.

Still other well-meaning owners embark on ambitious restorations they can't afford or can't handle and run out of money midstream, at which point they walk away and never come back.

Family farms often present situations where the original homeplace is no longer in use, while younger generations have built newer houses on the same farm. When that happens, the families begin using the old homeplace for storage. In those situations, broken and rotting windows, failing porches, and peeling paint are not necessarily a top priority, and thus the decline begins. And why would a farming family be inclined to sell the old place when it sits right in the middle of their still-thriving farm?

There are also cases where local government ordinances, code and zoning requirements, and even overzealous building inspectors have homeowners over a barrel, unable to sell or properly restore a place because of prohibitive restrictions that put the cost of restoration or adaptive reuse out of reach.

Absentee Owners

Not surprisingly, out of sight, out of mind is frequently at play with endangered structures. Maybe a surviving heir lives all the way across the country, routinely paying the yearly property taxes by mail without having set foot on the property in years.

> Not surprisingly, out of sight, out of mind is frequently at play with endangered structures.

As family farms continue to die out and their land is purchased by corporate farming entities headquartered hundreds of miles away, the old homeplace sitting in the middle of three hundred acres is of no concern to corporations, certainly not worth preserving, in their opinion. These entities lean more toward demolition, and why throw money at that when nature will eventually do the work for free? They simply plant crops right up to the doorstep and keep rolling. Contacting these corporations and making a convincing case for moving or dismantling and rebuilding an old house is a stretch at best.

Path of Progress

Historically, developers and state highway departments do not typically possess a track record of care and concern for old structures. With the exception of old graveyards, environmental issues, archaeological evidence of very early Native American activity, or only the most extreme and high-profile cases of historic significance, the "path of progress" usually wins the day without much of a fight. When these situations arise, it is usually left to the most passionate activists among us to chain ourselves to an old Corinthian column or stir up loud and nasty dust on social media and in the news—often with results that end up doing more harm than good.

Land Grabs

Land grabs with an old house standing in the way are also common. There was a recent case in a small South Carolina town—a business owner purchased an adjoining property, making heartfelt promises to the owners about how he wanted to protect the extremely significant historic house that stood there. The day after the sale, he brought in bulldozers and took the house down.

The Inevitable

Once an old house finds itself caught in one or more of the circumstances outlined here, the inevitable progression is not hard to predict.

Natural causes usually do the trick—water being the leading culprit. Vines and overgrowth can engulf a place seemingly overnight. Lightning, hurricanes, tornadoes, and even the weight of snow and ice can be enough to finish a place off.

Manmade causes also contribute. Vandals and vagrants sometimes inadvertently set places on fire. Arsonists, on the other hand, do the same thing on purpose. Sometimes, property owners give permission to local fire departments to burn old structures as training exercises for the firemen, not realizing there were other options available.

Conclusion

And that brings us to this sad fact: Many old houses simply die from lack of knowledge. We lose a lot of our best old places because homeowners are not aware that there is preservation help available. Even within many communities

> Many old houses simply die from lack of knowledge.

and municipal and county governments, there can be misunderstanding or a lack of awareness about private and public preservation tools that are already in place, much less a lack of knowledge of how to access and utilize that help.

As we move through this book, you will learn what that help looks like, where to find it, and what role it (and you!) can play in saving an old house from an undeserved fate.

2

IS IT REALLY PROTECTED?

Learning the Benefits and Limits of Historic Designations

"But this house was on the National Register of Historic Places. How could it have been torn down?" I have heard this question too many times for comfort. So, perhaps, have you. Maybe the words have come out of your own mouth. If so, you are not alone. Many years ago, I uttered them myself.

There are many common misconceptions about what constitutes protection for significant structures. Oftentimes, those misconceptions serve as detriments to our historic houses because the only ones outside of preservation circles who are well acquainted with the ins and outs of our current system of preservation are the ones who have a vested interest in working around it—developers and commercial builders. The sad result is that these entities have learned how to take advantage of the public's general misconceptions when disposing of significant properties. The only real repercussions they have to deal with are local outcries after the fact, and those can't bring back what has just been destroyed.

Changing that dynamic begins with a basic understanding of the historic-preservation system and framework currently in place. Forthcoming chapters will take a more in-depth look at each component, but here we are at bird's-eye level, which is a helpful start.

There are three main levels of protection for a historic structure or site or district. These are overseen by both public/government agencies and private nonprofits. In order of the least protection to the most, they are as follows:
- National Register of Historic Places – minimal protection
- Local or State Historic Landmark – partial protection
- Preservation Easement with Protective Covenants – strongest protection

National Register of Historic Places
The National Register of Historic Places is an official list of the United States Federal Government. It was authorized in 1966 as part of the National Historic Preservation Act. Administered through the National Park Service via each state's Historic Preservation Office, National Register designations are awarded after a significant application process that involves, among other things, site analysis and comprehensive research into the historic and architectural context of the site. The applications are generally written by paid qualified consultants, and then a designation is either awarded or denied.

> The truth is that unless a National Register property is impacted by a state or federally funded licensed or permitted project, the National Register designation conveys very little protection.

Once a site is listed or included in a National Register Historic District as a contributing property, there are tax incentives that may be available. The State Historic Preservation Office in each respective state can provide details on how such incentives apply to the property in question.

While these designations are marks of the highest honor for a property, they carry with them little to no protection against harm or demolition. This comes as a surprise to many, but the truth is that unless a National Register property is impacted by a state or federally funded licensed or permitted project, the National Register designation conveys very little protection.

Local or State Historic Landmark

Most county governments and all state-level governments have entities dedicated to the preservation of historic structures and sites. These groups typically have authority that goes beyond what National Register designation can accomplish.

At the state level, they are called the State Historic Preservation Office, or SHPO, commonly referred to as "Ship-O."

Many individual counties within a state also have commissions, appointed by county governments. The names of county-level agencies can vary from state to state and county to county but are frequently known as Historic Preservation Commissions, or HPC, which is the case where I live in North Carolina.

By law, these various agencies are empowered to enact certain restrictions and penalties against harmful treatment or demolition of historic structures by granting landmark status to a property, either as a local or a state historic landmark.

With these designations, which, again, are generally applied for using a paid consultant to prepare a report similar in nature to a National Register application, comes a significant reduction in annual property taxes—for instance, 50 percent in North Carolina—in exchange for which the property owner agrees to abide by the guidelines enacted through the state or local entity granting the designation.

These guidelines can vary from one county to the next, and even from state to state, but they generally carry very specific stipulations about proper procedures for restoration, renovation, and repair that closely follow the Secretary of the Interior's Standards for the Treatment of Historic Properties. Failure to follow the guidelines can result in denial of a requested permit for which work on the landmark structure is proposed or, in some cases, even a revocation of the property tax abatement.

Most all of the SHPOs and HPCs can also place a moratorium on proposed action against a landmark property, typically for a set period of time, during which time there are stiff penalties if a property owner violates the moratorium.

While all of these steps certainly help to protect historic structures, they are not absolute deterrents against harm. A determined developer, for instance, can simply run out a clock on a moratorium if the eventual financial payoff is attractive enough. So, too, can a determined new property owner in a case such as a land grab, where the new owner is only interested in the land.

Preservation Easements With Protective Covenants

For obvious reasons, the United States lags behind much older regions of the world in terms of preservation efforts. By virtue of age alone, some of our oldest structures here would be considered mere youngsters in Europe and elsewhere, and yet we historically are much too quick to deem a structure "too old to fool with." The result has been the loss of a large chunk of America's architectural history.

> During the twentieth century, however, heavily aided and abetted by our national bicentennial celebration, there began to be an awareness of the need for an organized and systematic approach to preservation.

During the twentieth century, however, heavily aided and abetted by our national bicentennial celebration, there began to be an awareness of the need for an organized and systematic approach to preservation. Therefore, in addition to the national, state, and county efforts already mentioned, many private nonprofit organizations were born, dedicating themselves to the specific task of saving what remained.

Today, many of these nonprofits operate statewide, while others confine themselves to major metropolitan areas, areas of broad historical significance, or specific counties or municipalities, but all of them are dedicated to the premise of historic preservation and empowered to help through their various charters.

Through the years, these private efforts have helped to define and develop what are today known as preservation easements and protective covenants or other such preservation agreements. To quote my friend, Myrick Howard, President Emeritus of Preservation North Carolina, "Preservation easements are the strongest tool in the preservation tool belt."

Easements and covenants are legally binding, permanent, and carry stiff penalties when breached that can range from financial fines to even revocation of ownership in extreme cases.

They are enacted at the request of, and with the consent of, property owners by way of legal documents that outline the specific stipulations and protections for a property. These documents, once executed, attach to the deed in perpetuity and remain in effect even when the property changes hands, affecting all successive future owners.

Easements and covenants are flexible and can be customized to each property, with some dictating stipulations for exterior only, while others touch on important interior features as well. Additionally, there can be clauses addressing significant auxiliary features beyond the main structure, and even language concerning certain trees and landscape features. Simply put, whatever need and willingness exists, an easement or covenant can be crafted to cover and protect it.

Enforcement

It would be nice to imagine that we found the magic preservation bullet the day the first preservation easement was placed on a property, but the truth is that all of these layers of protection are only as strong as the entities charged with enforcing them.

Enforcement involves oversight, which is time consuming and expensive. Government agencies are not set up for the kind of detailed scrutiny required to monitor every single property under their purview. And even the most broadly staffed, flush-with-cash private nonprofits have manpower limits.

No one can be everywhere at once, but the hopeful news is this: Increased public awareness and understanding of how the system works can exponentially expand the power of the systems that are in place. Even when a nonprofit or government agency cannot keep check, informed local eyes can. They—we—can be effective boots on the ground, passing a timely word to a jurisdictional entity when warranted.

But we can only be as effective as the knowledge we possess. Hopefully this chapter has provided a basic understanding of our current preservation framework, a productive first step. Before we move into a deeper look at each piece of that puzzle, however, our next chapter will take a look at the economic, cultural, and quality-of-life benefits that historic preservation brings to the table.

3

WHY BOTHER?

Preservation's Long List of Benefits

Common thinking tells a lot of people that it makes more economic, environmental, and practical sense just to tear an old house down.

"Bring in the bulldozers. It is nothing but a money pit, impossibly expensive to restore, trouble waiting to happen down the line." In short, most of the time we say, "Why bother?"

Unpacking that perspective, however, reveals an entirely different set of answers that may surprise you.

Let's Start with the Beloved Bulldozers

Who loves a good landfill? Outside of demolition contractors, no one raises a hand. But that is where old houses end up. This may be one of those things you knew but never really thought about. Those mountains of debris aren't just made up of your old coffee grounds and empty cans of beans. Our landfills are also comprised of construction debris in significant quantities. Looked at from that angle, saving a structure from demolition is recycling at its finest.

> Saving a structure from demolition is recycling at its finest.

Also consider what we are saving. Old houses are made of old-growth wood from large trees—a superior product whose density and strength far outshine rushed-to-market wood. By comparison, today's construction industry is a beast that consumes and demands more at an alarming rate. And beyond the wood, we routinely throw away natural stone, hand-formed bricks, early glass, slate and copper roofing, and more. All of these materials are either difficult to replicate or prohibitively expensive. And for every old house that does manage to get the benefit of an architectural salvage operation before demolition, there are a hundred whose executioners could care less.

Money Pit or Treasure Chest?
This depends on whether or not you believe a glass to be half empty or half full. Repairing wide-plank flooring with matching reclaimed wood from the same period is not cheap, for instance. Neither is patching a slate-tiled roof. Rebuilding an existing wood-frame window costs money, as does the proper repair of plaster walls, and on and on. That's the glass half empty. In the half-full category, however, lies the assessment of what you will have when completed, and just as importantly, what is still in good shape, still holding value, and won't need attention. The sum total of all the parts and the end result is a structure of enduring quality and design that stands head and shoulders above its newer counterparts.

Investing in a proper renovation/restoration on the front end will yield ongoing financial rewards that make the effort worthwhile. And in the process, an existing structure has been saved, which means no new trees had to be cut, no asphalt shingles had to be manufactured, one less set of worn-out vinyl windows will be going to a landfill, and the giant oak in the front yard will live to shade several more generations, having been saved from the clear-cutting that developers say they cannot live without.

Gentlemen, Start Your (Economic) Engines
Saving old structures provides inherent economic benefits for the communities, towns, and counties involved. A great example in North Carolina is the case of Glencoe Village—an abandoned mill village with dozens of empty and endangered old houses. As it stood, the derelict nature of

the place had reduced the tax value down to not much more than the value of the land it occupied. Enter Preservation North Carolina, who decided to undertake and spearhead the task of bringing Glencoe back from the brink. Today Glencoe is once again a thriving community filled with houses whose tax value far exceeds the land around it. These were not grand dwellings—George Washington never slept there—but they were well-built structures with potential. That was reason enough to preserve them.

Another very tangible benefit of preservation is the contagious nature of success and what that can mean for a community. Once people see with their own eyes how the saving of old places actually brings fresh financial life to a neighborhood, more and more become willing to save them.

> Saving old structures provides inherent economic benefits for the communities, towns, and counties involved.

In turn, increased preservation activity often spawns the formation of revolving funds, which are pools of investment money, both private and public. Investors use these funds to underwrite projects, sell them at a profit with protective covenants to ensure their longevity, and then plow those profits back into the revolving fund for the next project.

Why Bother? The Better Question Is Why Not?
I have only touched on a few of the benefits of historic preservation in this chapter. There are many more. When viewed, however, through just about any lens available—whether historic, cultural, economic, environmental, artistic, or academic, to name a few—the answer is clear: When we make the effort to save what remains, everyone wins.

4

WHERE CAN I FIND HELP?

Learning the Preservation Landscape

Witnessing the slow deaths of worthy old houses is a familiar routine for many of you. With no idea of where to begin to find help, you resign yourself to one day driving past and finding the old place in a heap on the ground.

In this chapter, we will take a look at the step-by-step checklist that can guide you to two things—determining property ownership and going through available channels to seek help. In the end, discovering such information may prove pivotal to the future health and safety of some of these properties.

An Important First Step
Start by finding out who owns the property in question. This can be done through your local county tax office, with staffers willing to help you identify a property owner and furnish you with contact information at least in the form of a mailing address. This is important as a first step because without a willing owner, there is no point in further pursuing the preservation. If, however, you discover an owner who is as desperate to find a solution as you are, then you have just made a friend, and one plus one equals a team. It's a start.

GRASSROOTS GUIDE TO SAVING WHAT MATTERS

The Big Picture

In general terms, there is a framework of preservation help here in the United States that exists in three layers:
- **Local Help:** county historic-preservation commissions, private local groups dedicated to historic preservation, designated historic districts, and regional groups dedicated to historic preservation
- **State Help:** state historic-preservation offices and state-level groups dedicated to historic preservation, and private foundations with grant money available
- **National Help:** the National Trust for Historic Preservation and private foundations with grant money available

This is the landscape upon which preservation efforts operate. Sometimes there is only local help involved (and sometimes that is enough). Other times, state-level help steps in as well. And there are occasions when a comprehensive effort from local all the way up to national ends up providing the solution.

Local Help

The logical starting place is local. These are the groups that comprise your boots on the ground. They are staffed and operated by local residents, many of whom are very familiar with the property in question. A county historic-preservation commission can provide you with information about getting the property designated as a local historic landmark. That is a good first step.

> A county historic-preservation commission can provide you with information about getting the property designated as a local historic landmark.

Another important step, when possible, is to reach out to a local preservation group to see if protective covenants or a preservation easement can be secured. Many such groups, including the county historic-preservation commissions, are set up legally to grant such protections—with the prior permission of the property owner. As we have already discussed, those protections are the best way to ensure the least amount of future harm. In rare cases, a city or a county can also be persuaded to step in with financial help if the property in question is of significant importance to the area.

State Help
Even when local help is available, there are times when a state-level group can come alongside with preservation advice or financial assistance. There are also many cases where local groups cannot grant easements or covenants, at which point statewide preservation nonprofits can accomplish those goals. Additionally, state historic-preservation offices have trained staff members qualified to give proper guidance and ensure that properties are handled according to accepted preservation standards. In some instances, properties and sites can receive designation by the state offices as State Historic Sites or Landmarks. Within each state, there typically resides one or more private foundations whose mission and focus are on funding, as opposed to granting protections. These groups form yet another arm of assistance by routinely funding preservation projects small and large.

National Help
Obviously, applying for a property to receive designation on the National Register of Historic Places cannot hurt, even though we have already outlined the limited protection such a designation offers. As well, entire streets, neighborhoods, and districts can apply for designation as National Register Historic Districts. This gives participatory designation to each contributing property within that district—again, largely honorary but still beneficial and desirable. Beyond this designation, however, there are cases where a property can be designated as a National Historic Landmark, a site can become a National Register Historic Site, and a district can become a National Register Historic District.

> There are many foundations and corporations who offer annual grants dedicated to historic preservation, often with a larger pool of capital from which to operate.

Private money is also available on a national level. There are many foundations and corporations who offer annual grants dedicated to historic preservation, often with a larger pool of capital from which to operate. Applying for and receiving grant money through these nationwide sources plays an integral role in preservation efforts—often making the difference between success and failure. A partial list of these resources is included at the end of this book.

5

GRANTS AND INCENTIVES

Funds Are Available If You Know Where to Look

The focus of this chapter is on projects owned by groups such as private nonprofits, churches, civic organizations, local governments, etc. If you are a private citizen seeking help for your own property, however, the information here can still be of use.

One of the most logical deterrents to any preservation effort is the matter of funding such a project. Almost by default, endangered structures are thought of as money pits. While not all of them deserve that extreme label, the truth is that money should be one of the first orders of business when faced with a project. Understanding the scope of the financial challenges ahead will ensure the best outcome. By the same token, failure to grasp reality beforehand can easily ensure failure. So getting a clear picture, from the outset, of potential monetary investment is not only helpful but also essential. Once you have a grasp (and take a few deep breaths), the journey can begin. With good luck and proper planning, success is very often the result.

A brief history concerning an 1817 Federal structure in North Carolina provides a hopeful case in point. It is the oldest brick building in my hometown of Lincolnton, North Carolina. Having been leased from

> Getting a clear picture, from the outset, of potential monetary investment is not only helpful but also essential.

the county for over a hundred years by the local United Daughters of the Confederacy (UDC) group, whose stewardship across the decades was commendable and kept the building alive, the structure nevertheless looked as if it was heading into endangered territory.

Twenty-two original windows and their wavy glass were in sad shape, several of them in danger of falling out into the street. Original lime mortar was crumbling between the handmade bricks. Interior plaster was falling off the walls. The greatest portion of the front-door surround had rotted and fallen away. Water and weather were taking a toll. And the conditions assessments with recommendations and estimates from qualified professionals had been prohibitively steep.

In spite of their success in years past regarding grants and funding, the UDC group found themselves at a dead end. The cost to restore and preserve the building was simply beyond their reach. With their blessing, and with the long-term survival of the structure at the forefront of their minds and ours, several concerned citizens formed a new local nonprofit group, Lincoln Landmarks, Inc., dedicated to historic preservation throughout the county. And working through Preservation North Carolina, we were able to purchase the building to serve as our headquarters and be open to the community for all to enjoy.

Along with that purchase came a commitment to a five-year plan of rehabilitation. The first order of business was, obviously, funding. Faced with the same assessments that had loomed over the previous owners, we decided to take one step at a time in order of priority. Early assistance from the city and the state provided enough seed money to ensure that the building was watertight and to have the windows rebuilt. Past that, we have now set our sights on repairing all of the crumbling exterior mortar, hopefully with the assistance of a grant that we have recently applied for. We were fortunate that the building was still structurally sound, but the work accomplished over the past two years came not a minute too soon. Along the way, we have gained memberships and sponsorships and will stage recurring fundraisers to keep the ball rolling. Bit by bit, the mountain that we faced is looming smaller each day.

One Bite at a Time

Approaching such projects on an incremental basis is important—especially when the task is large and complex. A former business mentor of mine was fond of quoting this favorite line: "How do you eat an elephant? One bite at a time." Attempting to fund a rescue in totality from the outset is a good way to talk yourself out of ever beginning.

> Take first steps first, find funding for each step as you go, and build a record of success.

Take first steps first, find funding for each step as you go, and build a record of success. In so doing, obtaining funds for future increments will be easier because the requests will be accompanied by a good track record of performance. Funding sources will take such things into account when considering your application. To put it another way, if you are hard at work hanging new drapes when there is a gaping hole in the roof, you will not be taken seriously. Get funding to secure the structure first, and *then* hang the drapes.

Finding the Funds

When you are new to the process, learning where grant and incentive money is to be found, applied for, and hopefully received is part of the learning curve. Just as we have already seen in previous chapters outlining the varying levels of help in protecting a historic structure, there are also sources of funding for preservation projects that track along the same lines—local, state, and national. There is also a fourth source—private funding from individuals.

Begin at Home

The most logical starting point in the search for funds is your own backyard, where local governments, preservation groups (if they exist in your town or county), and potential local donors will already be familiar with the site—especially if it holds important community significance. If your project is one that will be serving the public in some way, your chances increase. Even in small towns and less affluent areas, there is often city and county money earmarked for historic preservation (sometimes unknown to the public and sitting unused in the budget year after year), and even when not, town councils and county boards can be instrumental in creating such allocations. Likewise, local businesses are often willing partners in such projects in exchange for the good community PR and advertising opportunities they present. These kinds of charitable donations also help their corporate bottom line. Beyond local businesses, you may be fortunate enough to know of potential funds from private citizens with a track record of charitable donations to good causes. It never hurts to inquire.

Beyond Your Borders
In addition to local resources that have been put to use, there are funds available on a statewide level. All state governments, in partnership with the National Park Service/National Trust For Historic Preservation and acting through their state historic-preservation offices, annually grant money to various preservation efforts, both through their historic-preservation fund grants and their certified local governments grants.

As well, many private foundations grant money on a statewide basis. One such group in North Carolina is the Marion Stedman Covington Foundation, a group that has actively been funding historic preservation efforts since 1986. Searching online in your own state for comparable organizations can yield fruitful results. The Resource Guide at the end of this book will provide a good working list of as many online resources as possible, but in the meantime, if you are proficient with online search, loosen up those typing fingers and go searching.

Across the Nation
The National Trust for Historic Preservation, is of course, the nationwide leader of funding opportunities for historic preservation. Their website

gives a great overview of their vast landscape of opportunities, above and beyond the state-level grants mentioned above.

Another great nationwide resource is The 1772 Foundation, whose video on the advantages of The Revolving Fund is very informative.

Also granting preservation funds on a national level is The Daughters of the American Revolution, a.k.a. DAR.

More information about each of these resources can be found in the Resource Guide at the end of this book.

In Summary
By now I hope you are encouraged that there are hundreds, even thousands, of avenues to secure financial help for your preservation project. I have barely scratched the surface in this chapter. Indeed, there are entire websites that serve as vast databases of sources, providing links to multiple thousands of these grant opportunities. The most comprehensive of these charge a subscription fee for access, one such being HistoricFunding.com. As you can see on their home page, there is no shortage of help available. But whether you choose to invest in a subscription to one of these databases or simply want a few hints in the right direction via books such as this, I hope that you will not shy away from trying. That first step is the most important.

6
I JUST WANT TO SAVE MY HOUSE
Preservation Options for Homeowners

If you are the owner of a historic structure, you are already well aware that it was here long before you were and will likely be here long after you are gone. That is, at least, the hope. But what about that? Is your old house a survivor only because of good luck, or is it here because someone cared enough to ensure its survival via legal means of protection? The question strikes at the very heart of historic preservation, yet I continue to be amazed at the number of well-meaning and knowledgeable homeowners who have never given the matter much thought. They care deeply about their homes, can tell you all the ins and outs of their stories, have bent over backward to maintain and faithfully rehabilitate them at every juncture, but many folks simply assume or hope that the next stewards of their properties will go to the same lengths to protect them in the future as folks have in the past.

Familiar refrains I often hear include the following:

"My family has maintained this place for five generations. We will never sell it. My children and grandchildren will see to that." Unfortunately, squabbles among surviving children are more the rule than the exception, or heirs who inherit houses sometimes turn out not to care as much as their parents did. In both cases, an old house can, and often does, end up the victim.

"The house is on the National Register. We made sure to take care of that. The future is secure." National Register designation is a nice first step, but it holds virtually no protection, as we have already seen.

"The house is a historic icon. Who in their right mind would want to harm it?" Assuming the good will of a community toward a historic structure is also a thin limb upon which to extend one's hopes. There are indeed those "in their right mind" who would think nothing of demolition if the circumstance was conducive.

And last but not least, "We're going to donate this house and grounds to the county [or college, church, or other similar well-intentioned organization] after we are gone." While always a nice sentiment, donating a property to a government sometimes is the equivalent of unlocking the henhouse door and posting a sign that says, Welcome Foxes. Boards of commissioners and town councils change every few years, as do zoning laws and development ordinances, the sizes of county budgets, and political winds, and the list of perils goes on.

While none of these statements are unreasonable, they aren't safe bets either. Then again, you may be among those realists who say, "I know the pitfalls, and I worry about what will become of this place after I'm gone." If so, this chapter is for you.

The best answer to providing the highest level of protection is to secure protective covenants or a preservation easement for your home and property, two processes that are almost identical, and both of which will place restrictions on the deed to your property with very specific instructions about what can and cannot be done. As we have already seen, these documents are intended to be in effect in perpetuity or, in other words, pretty much forever—no matter who the future owners may be.

Legally binding, the covenants are typically granted—at your request, with your permission, and with your input as to what they contain—by any number of preservation organizations. Some of those are local nonprofits operating in your city or county, others are regional, and still others operate across entire states. Since these are legal documents, there is generally a fee associated with their preparation, but many organizations offer flexible solutions to make things easier. These organizations are, after all, in existence for just this purpose, and it is in their best interest to make the process as easy as possible for any homeowner willing to take the steps toward ensuring the future preservation of their home.

You can start the process of obtaining a preservation easement or restrictive covenants with a few basic inquiries about which organizations with the capacity to grant them are operating in your area. Once you identify your options, make sure you choose a strong organization with a long track record of stability. There is nothing binding about any of these steps until a document is actually signed and recorded, but making sure that you are going with an entity capable enough to maintain the oversight of your property for the long haul will enable you to enter such conversations with confidence.

In so doing, you will not be "donating" the property to anyone, nor will you be preventing it from going to your designated heirs, if there are any. You are simply creating legal protection for the house moving forward, regardless of the owner. Failure to abide by the terms of the covenants can result in financial penalties for an irresponsible future owner. As well, in extreme cases, some of these documents provide for the property to revert to the preservation organization itself, though those instances are rare. All told, however, taking these measures provides the highest level of legal protection for the future safety and integrity of a historic structure.

Along with the legal protection, securing a National Register nomination is a very high honor that adds heft to any preservation easement. Likewise, applying with your local government to have the property declared a local historic landmark is beneficial. In addition to your own protective covenants, local landmark designation often carries with it the previously mentioned right of local governments to place a 365-day stay on any intended adverse action to a local landmark property. And as we have seen, these designations can also bring with them a hefty reduction in yearly property taxes.

In summary, there are three very good things you, as a homeowner, can do to ensure future safe passage for your home:
1. National Register designation
2. local historic landmark designation
3. protective covenants/preservation easements

Our next chapter, "We Meant Well," will look at the preservation, rehabilitation, and restoration process and highlight many common mistakes made by homeowners who don't realize they are doing anything wrong until it's too late. And don't let that title dissuade you. We have all, at some point, inadvertently been guilty of some kind of preservation faux pas.

7

WE MEANT WELL

The Most Common Restoration and Rehabilitation Mistakes

This chapter will touch on a few important areas where well-meaning owners of historic homes make innocent mistakes during restoration and rehabilitation. This list is by no means comprehensive, but the mistakes are commonplace.

Replacement Windows

Three words can summarize this section: "Don't do it." Replacing handcrafted wood windows that still work with an aluminum- or vinyl-clad product is a mistake on at least two levels. First of all, replacement windows do not last forever and are not repairable, for the most part. This means they will, sooner rather than later, end up in a landfill, and the house will be back to square one, not to mention the landfill will have yet another pile of nonbiodegradable construction waste to deal with. Secondly, the design of replacement windows typically does not hold a candle to that of originals, and it will show—glaringly so.

But don't worry; there are better options available. For energy efficiency, there are inner liners that can be mounted to an original window on the inside—full sheets of glass with just a thin outer rim that fits snugly against the window to provide the needed insulated air pocket. Original windows can be rebuilt and also repaired. Original wavy glass is still available; frames, sashes, and muntins can all be rebuilt; and windows can be reglazed and repainted over and over again. That is how they have managed to last for the past two centuries intact.

Spray-Foam Insulation
Sealing an old house against moisture, tight as a drum, might seem like a great idea for heating and cooling, when in fact it could easily end up killing your house. Early designs were meant to allow a house to breathe, and the flow of air upward and out was an intended feature to provide natural ventilation and air flow. Completely watertight sealing in walls, foundations, around windows, etc. with modern spray-foam insulation can actually prevent a house from breathing, which in turns traps moisture in the walls and eventually rots studs, siding, window casings, and even foundation sills. If you want to improve the heating and cooling aspects of your old house, consult your state historic-preservation office. Most of those experts can either give you the proper guidance or put you in touch with someone who will.

Drywall Replacing Plaster
When at all possible, repair your original lime plaster walls with the same product. Properly handled, plaster walls will help retain the authenticity of your home—much in the same way proper handling of the finish on a fine antique helps hold the value, and improper refinishing can completely erase that value. Drywall can have the same effect when it is obviously replacing earlier and much more desirable plaster. By the same token, attempting to repair plaster by smearing the cracks with drywall mud is a recipe for disaster. The two materials are not compatible, and sooner or later, the "mud" will lift right off.

Modern Flooring

This one is so very tempting, but natural original flooring with no imperfections is not the aim when approaching the matter of floor restoration in an old house. If perfection is your goal, it may prove to be unattainable. All authentic old flooring contains imperfections. The end result should not look like a shiny and pristine gym floor. The home renovation experts on HGTV love coming in and doing an entire house in luxury vinyl tile or plank flooring. It can, they say, cover a multitude of sins. These replacements are durable, easy to clean, affordable, beautiful, and on and on.

> There is no substitute for the deeply layered beauty of original wood floors.

(What's more, the hosts neglect to mention that shortcuts allow them to cut to the chase and make their deadline for the show's film crew ....) Modern substitutions also seem like a great "cover-up" for the DIY homeowner who doesn't even know where to start in repairing or replacing original wood floors. But as beautiful and as practical as modern flooring is, there is no escaping the fact that it is new—and that takes us right back to the notion of mishandling an antique. There is no substitute for the deeply layered beauty of original wood floors, and help can be found if you are patient and diligent. Old flooring is frequently salvaged and made available for resale. The end result will be worth the effort.

Open Concept

What's not to love? If we are to believe every single thing we read online or see in the real estate listings or enjoy on cable TV, open concept is the only way to go. Today's families enjoy the convenience of living, cooking, dining, and entertaining in one large space. All well and good, but if your house is historic, then knocking out too many interior walls in the quest for open concept can actually rob the rooms of their proper due. Years ago in my capacity as a real estate broker, I was honored to have listed a grand 1817 Federal mansion—one of North Carolina's finest. One of my showings involved a young wedding and event planner who had plenty of money and not a lick of awareness of what she was seeing. After making a quick pass through the main floor with its grand fourteen-foot ceilings, finely wrought plasterwork ceiling medallions and crown moldings, large expansive rooms, and light-filled foyer, she came breezing out the door and said (while pecking on her phone), "So do you think the preservation people will let me gut the inside? I really do need open concept if I'm going to be having events here." Before I could stop them, the words were already tumbling out of my mouth, "This is not the house for you. Thank you for coming. Goodbye."

Standing Seam Metal Roofs
Be careful with this. Modern metal roofs do indeed look very close to their earlier authentic versions, and they are a great option for roofing, unless …

Color choice can make or break this decision, and the wrong choice can end up ruining the outward appearance of an otherwise very deserving old house. Any bright color should be avoided for a reason that many homeowners overlook—it will not age and fade with time. The fire-engine-red roof on your house will be the first and sometimes only thing people will notice. It will likely overshadow and overpower the structure itself and will still be doing so thirty years from now—long after your enthusiasm for fire-engine red has flown the coop. Faux copper is another lurking mistake. It will not age to a nice soft green patina like real copper will. Instead, the top of your house with its faux copper roof will shine like a bright new penny—forever—possibly even visible from outer space on sunny days.

Reproduction Trim Work
Very often, historic houses come on the market having been stripped of part (or all) of their original moldings, window trims, mantels, and even doors. A very common mistake during rehabilitation is to purchase modern reproductions as replacements. Sometimes made of molded resin or even hardened foam, but even when made of wood, these offerings rarely hold

a candle to the hand-carved and molded details they are replacing. The mass-produced products commonly found at big home-improvement centers and online are lacking in both depth and quality of detail and are easily spotted as subpar substitutions once they are installed. If you have a remnant piece of your original molding that can be used as a profile for a good craftsman to reproduce, or one remaining Greek Revival corner block or keystone medallion from an archway—even original photos if all else fails—then the money you will pay to have these elements faithfully replicated will be a very good investment. Another alternative is to search the many architectural salvage companies who save original parts and pieces from historic houses and resell them. They will have a good selection to choose from, and when they don't, they frequently network with other salvage companies that do. What's more, they can help guide you away from using elements that are not in keeping with the era of your house.

> A very common mistake during rehabilitation is to purchase modern reproductions as replacements.

Bricks and Mortar

If you are confronting repairs to exterior brick on walls and foundations, pay special attention to the type of mortar that was originally used. It likely was lime mortar, which is an entirely different product from today's modern mortar material. What's more, your existing mortar has aged over time. Authentic lime mortar is still readily available today in a wide variety of colors. Matching this to the old mortar on your project can produce repairs that are barely noticeable. And it goes without saying that every effort at brick replacement should include matching the new brick to the old brick—in both size and color—to the best of your ability. As an example, do not rely on a color photo in a catalog or a photo online to make such a decision. The safest method for matching brick color is to obtain actual samples and hold them against your existing brick.

Out-of-Character Additions and Embellishments

Understanding the specific characteristics of the architectural era during which your house was built will keep you from making embarrassing errors that will brand you as an amateur and your house as the unfortunate victim. Let's use Victorian gingerbread trim as an example. It does not belong as an embellishment on the porch columns of an 1810 Federal house built eighty years before gingerbread trim was even a twinkle in anyone's eye. Gothic windows do not belong on a Colonial saltbox. A two-car garage tacked onto the side of a Greek Revival makes no visual or historic sense either. In fact, additions of any kind should be placed on the rear of a structure when possible, especially when the structure bears purity of architectural form. Visible additions on the front or sides of a structure, when absolutely necessary, should be compatible in design while differentiating themselves from the original structure in order to avoid the impression that they are original to the structure. The aim is not to create a fake architectural history. Shutters, when used, should be functional, hinged shutters that actually can close up a window. Decorative shutters simply tacked to each side of a window are a modern invention.

> Additions of any kind should be placed on the rear of a structure when possible, especially when the structure bears purity of architectural form.

The list of these potential blunders is long enough for a chapter on its own, but these few examples hopefully give a sense of what to bear in mind. Pay close attention to roof pitch, window scale, and porch and entry style; all of these can be potentially expensive and embarrassing mistakes when added out of context. Local historic-preservation commissions, state historic-preservation offices, and local- and state-level preservation nonprofits, not to mention numerous books about period architecture online, can all serve a valuable purpose in helping to steer you away from a misstep.

When in Doubt

If you have embarked on a journey to bring a historic house back to life, a first rule of thumb is to acknowledge how much you don't know. Only a very small percentage of people have enough background in historic restoration and rehabilitation to sail through on their own steam. (For frame of reference, I am not one of them.) Begin each step by seeking to learn. Get advice, ask for help, educate yourself. This is not to say that every restoration needs to conform to the highest standards of the most informed purists among us. Floors are sometimes beyond help, drywall is sometimes the only option, and houses that originally did not contain bathrooms obviously need them now. In short, no one argues with the need for modern functionality in an old home. But taking care to keep authenticity where it can be kept and replacing it with the very best replacement option when it can't be saved will help ensure that a noble effort to save a deserving old house will have the happiest ending possible. Your years of hard work deserve no less.

> If you have embarked on a journey to bring a historic house back to life, a first rule of thumb is to acknowledge how much you don't know.

8

I JUST WANT TO SAVE MY TOWN

A Beginner's Guide to Starting a Preservation Nonprofit

When Miss Tillie Bond sold the Georgian woodwork in her house to a group from up North in the year 1918, the people of Edenton, North Carolina, decided it might be time to step in and save Cupola House before they woke up one morning to find the cupola missing.

In Miss Tillie's defense, times were hard. Her family, the Dickinsons, had held Cupola House for 141 years through good and bad, war and peace, and everything else in between. For whatever reason, she must have felt she had no choice but to convey the elaborate original (as in 1758) Georgian embellishments in the house to the Brooklyn Museum.

In as fine an example of making lemonade out of lemons as I can recall, her desperation spawned the formation in that same year of what eventually became the Cupola House Association (the first community preservation effort in the state), which went on to raise enough funds to purchase the house and save it for future generations.

Considering that this house is quite possibly North Carolina's finest early dwelling, Miss Tillie's despair turned out to be history's gain. Cupola House is today the star of the show in Edenton, which is no small matter, as Edenton is populated by dozens of "stars"—each one of them worthy of a standing ovation.

And of course you can visit, tour, and even enjoy the reproduction Georgian woodwork, thoughtfully replaced as part of the ongoing restoration of this stupendous old house. Those people in Brooklyn are still holding on to the originals, and while I'm sure Edenton would love to have them back—and they should be returned, in my humble opinion—Cupola House, it turns out, is doing just fine either way.

This story with the happy ending serves as inspiration for what can happen when a community pulls together in a determined preservation effort. Thanks to the early pioneering effort in Edenton, many communities across the state are fortunate today to have preservation nonprofit organizations in their own town or community. Perhaps you live in such a place. But if not, and if you have long felt the need for such an effort, this chapter will helpfully point you in the right direction.

Founding a private nonprofit preservation organization is not as difficult as one might imagine. It can begin on a simple basis—two or three people, perhaps more, deciding that the need is great and the time is right. Once that very low hurdle is passed, the next stop should be a visit with an attorney. Most all of them understand the legal basics of setting up a nonprofit, though I do provide a helpful money-saving tip later in this chapter. An attorney can guide you through the necessary steps and help you determine the answers to a few basic questions. Those steps, and the resulting documents, will form the basis of your group's official bylaws.

Following that, they will file your paperwork with your Secretary of State. You will also need to file paperwork with the IRS, requesting that you be granted official status as a nonprofit charitable organization. Your attorney will be able to take care of that as well. Keep in mind that there will be filing fees in both instances, which are typically affordable for fledgling organizations. Prior to filing, your attorney will be able to outline all of the related costs.

A helpful tip in your journey will be to find and work with an attorney who has previously helped form a preservation nonprofit. This is not to say that you need to find a specialist who works only with nonprofits;

I am not even sure such specialists exist. But if an attorney has assisted other nonprofits in the past, that fact could end up saving you a substantial amount in attorney's fees—and here is why.

> If an attorney has assisted other nonprofits in the past, that fact could end up saving you a substantial amount in attorney's fees.

Three years ago, I helped found the preservation nonprofit in my own county. In the process of formulating our bylaws, which typically involve a multipage document containing specific legally binding language, the attorney was able to use as a template the bylaws of a preservation nonprofit that she had assisted in forming in a nearby county. She first obtained permission from that group, and from there, we were able to quickly format our own bylaws with just a few necessary changes in the wording. This saved hours of work on the attorney's part, and her resulting fees were only a fraction of what they normally would have been.

Once the document is filed, you are free to begin your efforts. You are allowed to operate as a nonprofit from the first date of your filing the request with the IRS—even though their response to your request may be months away. Your attorney can explain this in detail.

From here, the real work begins, but take heart. Your mission is a worthy one, and if you are willing to stay the course, good things will result. Your group will elect officers, form a mission statement, seek members, announce a first meeting, and begin the work specific to the community in which you live.

There is one very important distinction to draw as you lay the foundation of your effort: Historic preservation is an endeavor separate and apart from the pursuit of history in general. That lane belongs to historical associations. These are the people who dedicate themselves to telling the history of a place, which entails much more than historic architecture and the pursuit of preserving it. Very often it is assumed that historical associations will take care of historic preservation—and sometimes they do that as part of their general overall mission—but sometimes they have no focused interest in the architectural preservation aspect of history. Therefore, the communities who have groups dedicated specifically to preservation are much more successful in their efforts to save what needs saving. Historic preservation requires concentrated attention, and that is best accomplished through a separate group. The good news is that both organizations can and do frequently work together as good community partners, forming a much more beneficial whole.

And finally, I encourage you to do your homework. Learn as much as you can about the other preservation groups operating near you. Seek out the most successful ones in your state, also, and delve into their mission statements, their publications, their websites, the way they promote events, and even the help they offer new groups such as yours. The preservation community is a nationwide family, with pockets in every state and in very many cities and towns. This network always stands ready to help guide and encourage and provide resources for a new neighbor, so take advantage. You can also avail yourself of any of the resource links I have provided here in the *Grassroots Guide*, and I hope you will.

> Communities who have groups dedicated specifically to preservation are much more successful in their efforts to save what needs saving.

Our next chapter will take a deeper look at how the consensus of a community can make a difference, not only in an overall preservation effort but also in the effort to save a single endangered structure. There are pitfalls to avoid and best routes to take toward that end goal.

9

STRENGTH IN NUMBERS

Harnessing the Power of Community

The phrases "more than one way to skin a cat" and "you can catch more flies with honey" have nothing to do with skinning cats and catching flies. They do, however, come to bear when the subject is persuasion and the goal is consensus.

As this relates to the process of historic preservation, I have come to realize through the years that the preservation community is populated with a good number of talented folks who have honed the art of persuasion. They understand that quiet conversation in the pursuit of positive results holds more power than the angry bullhorn in the town square. The latter may bring attention and attract a certain type of crowd, but more often than not, the brief storm that results blows through quickly, leaving nothing in its wake but a few downed tree limbs for all the noise it made. Better to create a slow, soaking rain that will nourish good seed and produce growth when the sun returns.

In that light, this chapter will look at productive ways to create a healthy and positive attitude toward historic preservation within a community.

Shine a Good Light
Unless there already exists a long-standing history of preservation in a community, the first order of business is to raise awareness. Many years

ago, school children were taught about the historic structures in their midst as part of local and state history—typically around grades four or five. For many, myself included, this was an early cornerstone of what later became a lifelong passion. We were inspired at a very young age to attach value to these places and the stories they held. What naturally followed was a desire to make sure they were protected. For whatever reason, recent generations have not been given that same foundation, making the uphill climb even more steep in areas where preservation awareness is lacking. Still, a great deal can be accomplished in a short period of time.

Positivity is a good starting point. Through whatever means available to you, whether a newly formed preservation nonprofit, a personal social media page, guest editorials in the local newspaper, or simply one-on-one conversation, find ways to highlight the historic structures in your area via an interesting story, a home tour, or a photo feature on social media. Look for opportunities to include historic sites in community events—chamber of commerce tours, school field trips, etc. And be sure to do your homework. Getting your facts straight is essential.

Use the Network

There are kindred spirits in every community for just about any cause, and historic preservation is no different. In fact, it is one area of interest that touches multiple groups of enthusiasts—architects, artisans, craftsmen, historians, designers, preservationists, antique dealers, gardeners, archaeologists, genealogists, photographers, artists, writers—historic preservation is a broad subject that can and does engage them all. When viewed in this light, the potential for growing a network of like-minded thinkers is strong.

If you have personal friends or business associates involved in municipal or county or state

> If you have personal friends or business associates involved in municipal or county or state government, take care of those relationships. Use your interactions with them to speak positively about preservation and raise awareness.

government, take care of those relationships. Use your interactions with them to speak positively about preservation and raise awareness. No need to overstate your case or become annoying, but establishing a track record as an effective and reasonable advocate carries a great deal of weight.

Additionally, a network need not be confined to your own borders. Many of my long-standing friendships and relationships have been formed through outreach on a state and national level to those within the preservation community. Social media is an excellent way to connect outside your own sphere of influence, providing a much broader field of knowledge from which to draw. The guidance and encouragement you receive from expanding your reach often proves invaluable.

Learn How to Navigate Social Media
It should be no surprise to anyone who has even an occasional interaction on social media that it has become the "land of contention" on just about any subject one cares to name. Truly, I have come to realize that a post as innocuous as "The sky is blue" holds as much potential for a detrimental firestorm as one that advocates for abuse of the elderly (and in case you are wondering—no, I have never, ever posted on social media in defense of elder abuse!). Simply put, if you want to be taken seriously as a strong and respected advocate for historic preservation, learn how to behave yourself on social media.

The temptation to vent and rant in public and in writing can be very strong when you believe the cause is worthy enough. And certainly the recent demise of an old house that need not have died, or the impending endangerment of one, can tempt even the most restrained among us. This, however, is where careful steps need to be taken. My opening reference in this chapter to the angry bullhorn in the town square was not without cause. I have personally witnessed ill-advised social media posting regarding an endangered property descend into the worst sort of name-calling and vitriol, usually by those who have no dog in the hunt but thrive on finding a good argument on social media and jumping in with fists flying, even if they have no knowledge of the subject at hand. The end result is almost always a painful stalemate littered with a few of those aforementioned downed tree limbs, the thunder and lightning having moved on to the next juicy online argument, and the endangered house is still endangered ... and now surrounded by a lot of hurt feelings and misconceptions. Moral of the story: Don't go there.

The good news is there is a productive approach on social media that can be very effective in helping to spread the preservation message. Create posts that are uplifting. Look for stories, situations, and photos that bring good news, impart value, or inspire positive action. Even when the outlook is bleak and there is no other choice but to speak, do so *softly*. To the best of your ability, state your case with wording that does not provoke or get personal but instead provides a positive approach to solving the issue at hand. And monitor all of the resulting comments for a negative or detrimental turn of the conversation. Be especially vigilant for comment threads that take a turn against local officials. Whether you agree with these officials or not, they are very often the decision makers responsible for a good outcome. If your social media page has been the site of a large and out-of-control hate fest against a local board, such a thing could easily come into play at decision time. Better to take a post down than to allow it to jump the rails and do more harm than good.

> To the best of your ability, state your case with wording that does not provoke or get personal but instead provides a positive approach to solving the issue at hand.

Pick Your Battles

Not every preservation hill is worth dying on, as much as I wish that were not the case. If I could, I would save every last historic splinter. The realistic goal, however, is to make the list of those lost as short as possible.

Once you have built a strong community consensus around the need for historic preservation, that task becomes easier. The local "grapevine"—a.k.a. your network of trusted advocates—will help keep an eye on emerging situations that may call for action, such as a recently deceased homeowner with no heirs, a dire financial situation that threatens the future of a structure, a planned highway project that will be coming too close for comfort, or even a recent buyer of a historic property who is ready to sell and move on. Early warning signs here can make all the difference, so be alert and proactive for signs of pending activity.

Advance notice provides time for research, strategizing, and assessing whether the battle is winnable. General rules of thumb in this and all group pursuits are also good to remember. Choose words and actions carefully, don't burn bridges, stay on the high road, avoid drama, stay off of social media if possible, and seek solutions that offer some form of a win-win for all involved. During your assessment, don't make assumptions about a situation based on local anecdote or gossip. Instead, endeavor to speak directly with a property owner. You may be surprised to learn that local anecdote had it all wrong. When permissible, initiate low-key conversations with the government officials and boards who will be involved in the decision-making process and state your case, armed with the facts and a large contingent of local influencers in your corner.

Handled in this way, a good outcome and a happy ending for a structure or a site is much more likely, proving, I suppose, that there actually is more than one way to skin a cat, and flies really do flock to honey.

10

MORE THAN ONE WAY TO STOP A BULLDOZER

Ordinances and Statutes with Real Teeth

As we have progressed through this book on a practical approach to historic preservation, we have identified various proactive steps that can be taken to ward off demolition—the worst-case scenario for an old house. Even though neglect, misunderstanding of alternative options, and acts of nature are the star culprits when it comes to losing our old places, there is also the big elephant in the room: a developer's bulldozer.

How can one not feel helpless to act when it appears that forces far more powerful and well-connected have somehow taken control of a parcel that contains a significant old historic structure soon to be torn down? This situation, above all others, sometimes prompts even the most restrained among us to chain ourselves to a spectacular old Corinthian column and grab the infamous "angry bullhorn in the town square" to sound the alarm. Sadly, sometimes that is our only option. And sometimes it works.

There are, however, tools of last resort that reside in local ordinances and state statutes that can provide a legal route to buying valuable time. In some cases, they will stop the demolition process altogether. Because these are little known and rarely used, however, they can be completely passed over and never brought to bear in the very situations for which they were created.

As mentioned earlier in this book, local Historic Preservation Commissions reside in nearly every county of every state. These groups are typically appointed by the local boards of county commissioners and have the authority to place a 365-day hold on impending demolition or moving of a structure if it is a locally designated historic landmark or falls within a designated historic district. While not a permanent save, a full year may buy enough time for local concerned citizens and preservation groups to come up with a plan B. In my state of North Carolina, the name of that governing statute is NCGS 160D. This statute provides the same protection for structures listed on the National Register of Historic Places if they are shown on the nomination form as having statewide or national significance.

> If you can afford to do so, hire an attorney to research this for you, as they know where and how to search and what to look for.

Another option in the face of a proposed development is to check and see if the project has requested or been granted state or federal funds. If this is the case and the project contains a National Register property or district, or if the structure is a contributing property within a district (meaning it is listed as one of the structures within a National Register district), then there is a measure of protection provided through two reviews—the Section 106 environmental review process and the Section 4(f) review for transportation projects. In either or both of these cases, the developers may be required to take measures to mitigate any adverse impact. If you feel strongly enough about the need for either of these measures, reaching out to the SHPO office in your state might a good first step. That office can either give you advice on how these reviews are triggered and what they entail or, at the very least, can direct you to a local resource in your city or county for the same type of help.

Some communities enact local preservation zoning overlays that might afford some limited protection, so check with your municipal and county entities to see what ordinances are on the local books in that regard. Better yet, if you can afford to do so, hire an attorney to research this for you, as they know where and how to search and what to look for. You (or your attorney) may also be able to do deed research on properties in historic neighborhoods or other stand-alone properties just to see if there are any preservation easements or protective covenants that were placed on a property years ago but now mostly forgotten.

There are a few places where ordinances exist requiring demolition companies, heavy-equipment operators, salvage companies, etc. to wait a certain period of time before a permit can be granted. During the interim, public notice can be given that a permit has been applied for, providing time for parties with vested interests to take action.

In the midst of all this, seeking to keep an open line of communication with a developer is always a good-faith gesture. Many developers are not averse to allowing a structure to be moved, for instance. They are, after all, not really interested in the joy of destruction (unless we're talking about large mature trees, and don't get me started on that). In most all cases where old structures are concerned, a developer simply has a business to run, and things often stand in their way. If a qualified buyer can be found to pay for the cost of moving and thereby saving the structure, then everyone is happy. You may be surprised to learn that many important historic buildings do not sit where they were originally built and, for whatever reason, have been moved to other sites.

> You may be surprised to learn that many important historic buildings do not sit where they were originally built and, for whatever reason, have been moved to other sites.

One famous example of a building move is the historic Cape Hatteras lighthouse in North Carolina, which was moved 2,900 feet inland in 1999 as a future defense against the encroaching Atlantic Ocean. Other instances include Madison, Georgia's historic Heritage Hall, an 1811 structure that was moved 200 feet in 1909 to make way for a church parking lot, and the John Wright Stanly house, circa 1779–1783, which was moved from

Middle Street to George Street in New Bern, North Carolina, in 1966 to become a house museum as part of the Tryon Palace Complex.

These same developers may also be persuaded to save the "house that is in the way" for their own use in the proposed project, perhaps as a community center or some other purpose. Persuading a developer that he can have his cake and eat it too—i.e., successfully complete his project and come off as the white knight who saved an important old structure—may not be as difficult as one might imagine. Many of them never trouble themselves to learn the benefits of adaptive reuse unless the concept is brought to their attention as a possible solution to what might turn into a roadblock for their project. In some cases, they suddenly have open ears.

Finally, if all else fails, legal action may be advisable. This depends, of course, on whether or not there is a legal case to be made and whether or not those bringing suit have the money to do so. Very often, neither of these applies, but legal action should not be ruled out as an option. A preliminary conversation with an attorney to determine options in such cases would be a good first step.

Suffice to say, there are tools at our disposal short of forming a loud, raucous picket line around an old house (though I have been sorely tempted on occasion). With a bit of research, determination, and good luck, there just may be another way.

11

THE ART OF WIN-WIN

Turn a Developer into an Old House Enthusiast

By nature, developers generally are not fond of old houses. Their end goal is the bottom line. As this pertains to building large tracts of new homes, they perpetually seek the path of least resistance. Most large-scale developers are extremely adept at knowing how to steer a project through the labyrinthine landscape of permitting, zoning, and approvals. Many of them hire facilitators whose stated task is to act as liaison with local officials but whose real job is "Get it done. Make it happen no matter what."

And once the green light is given, the bulldozers roll. Trees that took a century to grow are cut down in minutes, felled by specialized pieces of heavy equipment fitted with giant hedge trimmers the size of SUVs. With one snap of those "scissors," a trunk is severed and the tree is on the ground. Enter the stump removers, followed by the haulers, then the graders, and from one day to the next, smooth bare dirt stands where a small forest once lived.

A project manager for one of the nation's largest homebuilders explained it to me this way: "It isn't the trees we mind; it's their roots. Roots are a builder's worst enemy. We can always plant new trees—and we do." Well, yes, if they want to call a little wimpy (and apparently invasive)

Bradford pear a tree, they technically meet the bare minimum criteria, but I'm not impressed.

> It is possible to make a case that saving the old house for adaptive reuse can actually benefit a developer's bottom line, not to mention his project.

In such an environment, then, how does an old house stand a chance? Why should the man who thinks nothing of mowing down a forest give a second glance to saving the old house that once stood at the center of the one hundred acres he's so happily scraping clean to the bone? As unlikely as that seems, it can happen. Depending on the circumstance, and on the stars aligning just so, and on the integrity of the developer in question, it is possible to make a case that saving the old house for adaptive reuse can actually benefit a developer's bottom line, not to mention his project.

Selling a developer on the idea of preservation and rehabilitation can require more than one approach. A good "salesman" can use them all and make it sound like the deal of the century—but do not despair if this is not in your wheelhouse. Even a quiet conversation centered around common sense can do the trick because the benefits are many.

Saving an old property helps the environment by reducing the amount of construction debris in landfills. Preservation also reduces time spent on site preparation and results in savings in labor and materials. The cost to stabilize and rehabilitate the structure is offset by the future use of the place as an integral and functional piece of the project. What's more, once they are stabilized, maintenance on these structures is no more difficult than maintenance on new construction. And, best of all, these places are often turned into centerpieces for the community being planned around them. They can become community centers, offices, educational spaces, coffee shops, fitness centers, spas, resource centers, and more.

Marketing and branding advantages can serve as built-in assets for a developer. If the house was well-known, or the family who owned it was prominent or held deep roots in the community, then the name of the house or the family can be incorporated into the name of the community itself—Elmwood Farm, The Village at Elmwood, etc.—providing a tangible sense of place and depth of history that would otherwise just be a manufactured name on a sign.

All of these advantages and more can help sway a developer—especially if he is just beginning the process of gaining permits and approval for his project. He can use his intent to save and repurpose as a selling point himself as he states his case to the various agencies.

Obviously, the best outcome for an old house is never to find itself in such a predicament. The highest and best future for these old places is that they, and as much of the land around them as possible, be saved from any developer's plans. But if your community finds itself in a situation where the health and well-being of a worthy old structure is at stake *and the sale of the property has already been accomplished*, then taking this route is the logical next step. There are no guarantees, of course, but the possible end result is certainly worth the effort.

You will have successfully turned a developer into an old house enthusiast, saved an old house, and created a win-win for all concerned.

12

IF EUROPE CAN DO IT

Why Our Old Houses Are Not Too Old

Maybe it is the relative youth of our nation, or our disposable culture, or something else entirely—but somewhere along the way, we have come to the mistaken belief here in the United States that anything much past one hundred years old is "too old to save." A brief word about that might serve a good purpose for those among us who throw up their hands in despair at the sight of a peeling coat of paint and a few rotten boards.

With so many renewable resources at our fingertips through the centuries, it has seemed much more expedient for us just to tear down and start fresh. If we trashed the old wood, there was plenty more where that came from, and plenty of room for hauling off and dumping, and a wealth of good builders raring to get going on the next thing.

It has only been within the last seventy-five years or so that the notion of respecting, saving, and preserving has come into play. Thankfully, men like John D. Rockefeller saw the value of taking fading and shabby towns like Williamsburg, Virginia, and bringing them back to life. We formed a National Trust for Historic Preservation, and we began paying attention. Gradually, the old houses among us came into proper focus.

Still today, though, we find ourselves battling the notion of "demo day" on cable TV, which does nothing much for the notion of respect for old houses, even though some of what ends up in those dumpsters is made of particleboard and likely belongs there.

But the problem is real. In order to counter the "too old" mindset, it occurs to me that taking a moment to consider the houses and villages around the rest of the world, Europe in particular, can bring a fresh frame of reference for what is truly old. Some of the houses in Europe were already centuries old before the first settler ever set foot on our continent, much less laid the first brick. And many of those houses still stand today and are still serving the purposes for which they were built. Not only are they alive and well, but so are their stories. When held up against this, our old houses are just beginning to show their age.

> Some of the houses in Europe were already centuries old before the first settler ever set foot on our continent, much less laid the first brick.

Given that, what do we have to whine about? Not that the preservation framework in European countries is perfect or a well-oiled machine, because each nation has their own individual hurdles to deal with, but as a whole, they are living proof that preservation is not only a worthy cause but a pursuit with results that are absolutely attainable and sustainable.

And that should bring comfort to anyone who cares about saving these places. If Europe can do it, so can we, and so we should.

13

WHAT NOW?

Options for Putting Preserved Structures to Work

This book bears a cover photo of the Bellamy Mansion in Wilmington, North Carolina, as it stands today, fully rehabilitated and serving to enhance the quality of life in this historic port city. Thankfully, Bellamy is currently under the expert care and stewardship of Preservation North Carolina—open to the public as a house museum and educational venue.

But what happens if, for whatever reason, the outcome cannot include such a great end result? What if a house can no longer be viable as a residence? What if, God forbid, the house really cannot be saved? Even then, there are options. Though they may not be optimal, they are better than demolition. That is the subject of this chapter.

> What if, God forbid, the house really cannot be saved? Even then, there are options.

In a perfect world, the surroundings of a historic house would remain the same as when it was built, but our world isn't perfect. These days, there may be a dual-lane highway where the front lawn used to be, or a tire-recapping service right next door. Even worse, an old mansion might find itself surrounded by four hundred brand-new rooftops built, miraculously, over the course of six short months, with not a tree in sight in any direction.

In these cases and more, those who manage to secure safe passage for a significant structure might find themselves face to face with a new reality. Not unlike the puppy who chased the car down the street and suddenly caught it, the matter of what comes next begins looming large.

The best solution, when use as a residence is no longer feasible, is to keep the integrity of the place while finding a new use. This is known in preservation circles as adaptive reuse or repurposing, and it can take many forms. One such house in Brunswick, Georgia, has found several new lives since it ceased being a residence many years ago. For a while, it contained a furniture store. And these days it is the very striking home of a local law firm.

Beyond office uses, these places hold great potential as restaurants and tea rooms, small boutique hotels, event venues, city clubs, headquarters for private nonprofits, upscale apartments, galleries, cultural centers, and more. And in newly developed settings, the old mansion in the middle can serve as a wonderful anchor—a restaurant, headquarters for the HOA, or even the center gathering spot of the neighborhood surrounded by parks, a pool, community gardens, or walking trails. It can serve as the community center, business center, fitness center, or all of the above.

Such adaptive reuse in these various forms has a proven track record of improving quality of life as well as the tax base and economic health of the community. Failing all of this, however, there is still hope.

Options for Saving What Can't Be Saved
Though it breaks my heart to witness it, there are rare cases when the only option is demolition. If the structure cannot be moved, adapted for a new purpose, or otherwise saved because of terminal structural issues, the next step is usually to call in the heavy equipment.

And here is where, if we are not vigilant, the last best option for an old place is completely overlooked. Just because the structure itself is past hope does not mean that the individual parts and pieces are worthless.

Think for a moment about a house filled with half a dozen ornate mantels, deep crown moldings, chair rails, wainscoting, stair risers, spindles, windows with original wavy glass, wide plank floors, paneled doors, original hinges and door locks, cornices, corbels, brackets, and pediments. Now imagine three scenarios.

Scenario One: A bevy of fire trucks rolls up, and half a day later, all of this is reduced to a pile of smoldering ash after an intentional controlled burn so that firefighters can receive valuable training.

Scenario Two: Bulldozers come in and erase decades, if not centuries, of historic architecture to a pile of rubble in a matter of hours.

Scenario Three: Salvage crews are allowed into the house to carefully remove as much of the historically significant interior as possible, and *then* the fire trucks or the bulldozers arrive. The firemen will *still receive* their much-needed training, or the bulldozer guy will *still earn a nice day's pay*, but an entire houseful of wonderful artifacts will live to see new life in another structure somewhere—either as replacement parts and pieces for a restoration of the same period or as nice historical touches in a new "old" house.

I will refrain from telling you how many significant pieces of architectural salvage end up falling prey to a fireman's torch or a wrecking ball simply because no one took the time to say, "Wait—is there anything we can save?" Suffice it to say, that number will break your heart.

14
SAVE THIS LIST
A Resource Guide for Homeowners

When I began writing this book, the intent was to bring practical information on saving historic architecture to those of us who care deeply about endangered properties but have no clue regarding where to begin, much less how to proceed from there. Very few of us have backgrounds in preservation, and without that, navigating the landscape is difficult. It seemed to me that a road map for the rest of us was in order.

And now that we have established that, a useful list of sources might help boost your newfound base of knowledge. Whether you are in need of a consultant to help you apply for a National Register of Historic Places designation or someone to restore old windows, the following may help get the ball rolling.

This list includes several nonprofit organizations who have assembled lists of service providers to the preservation industry and historic homeowners. Their lists include many categories—architects, architectural historians, preservation consultants who can write grant applications and nomination forms, archaeologists, window experts, masonry and plaster experts, decorative painters, stained glass artisans, suppliers of architectural salvage, artisan carpenters, and even general contractors.

While there are many more resources available, these should provide a good start.

By now, however, I trust that you know a bit more than you did when you opened this book. If it has inspired or encouraged you in any way, or helped to facilitate the preservation of a deserving old structure, then the effort has been worth it.

The National Park Service/National Trust for Historic Preservation:
https://www.nps.gov/subjects/historicpreservationfund/grant-programs.htm

Historic Preservation Fund Grants:
https://www.nps.gov/subjects/historicpreservationfund/grant-programs.htm

Certified Local Governments Grants:
https://www.nps.gov/subjects/clg/index.htm

Marion Stedman Covington Foundation:
https://www.mscovingtonfoundation.org

National Trust for Historic Preservation Grant Opportunities:
https://savingplaces.org/grants

The 1772 Foundation:
https://www.1772foundation.org

The Revolving Fund Explained:
https://www.youtube.com/watch?v=3Jo9PEY1h20

The Daughters of the American Revolution:
https://www.dar.org/national-society/dar-historic-preservation-grants

Historic Funding:
https://historicfunding.com

National Register:
https://www.nps.gov/subjects/nationalregister/how-to-list-a-property.htm

* Local Historic Landmark Designation:
https://www.hpo.nc.gov/local-preservation/local-historic-property-designations-north-carolina

* Protective Covenants/Preservation Easements:

https://www.presnc.org/get-help/easements-covenants/

* Please note these links pertain to North Carolina, where I live, but each should provide enough information to help you locate similar help in your own state.

Follow me online for daily and weekly updates and posts about historic preservation, insiders' guides to finding the best photo opportunities for old homes, endangered property alerts, and observations about life in the South.

Southern Voice Website: https://southernvoice.substack.com
Facebook: @BethYarbroughSouthernVoice

www.ingramcontent.com/pod-product-compliance
Lightning Source LLC
Chambersburg PA
CBHW030005050426
42451CB00006B/120